D0712975

SCIENTIFIC RIVALRIES
AND SCANDALS

WAR

OF THE
CURRENTS

THOMAS EDISON
VS NIKOLA TESLA

STEPHANIE SAMMARTINO MCPHERSON

Twenty-First Century Books
Minneapolis

To my husband, Dick

Thanks to Peg Goldstein for her insightful comments and editing, Steve Shegedin for helping with technical details, and Richard McPherson for his unfailing support and encouragement

Copyright © 2013 by Stephanie Sammartino McPherson

Twenty-First Century Books
A division of Lerner Publishing Group, Inc.
241 First Avenue North
Minneapolis, MN 55401 U.S.A.

Website address: www.lernerbooks.com

Library of Congress Cataloging-in-Publication Data

McPherson, Stephanie Sammartino.
    War of the currents : Thomas Edison vs Nikola Tesla / by Stephanie Sammartino McPherson.
       p. cm. — (Scientific rivalries and scandals)
    Includes bibliographical references and index.
    ISBN 978-0-7613-5487-1 (lib. bdg. : alk. paper)
      1. Electrification—History—Juvenile literature.
2. Electric currents, Alternating—Juvenile literature.
3. Electric currents, Direct—Juvenile literature. 4. Tesla, Nikola, 1856–1943—Juvenile literature. 5. Edison, Thomas A. (Thomas Alva), 1847–1931—Juvenile literature. I. Title.
TK1001.M37 2013
333.793′2—dc23   2011045526

Manufactured in the United States of America
1 – MG – 7/15/12

CONTENTS

LIGHTING
THE WHITE CITY

No one who witnessed the opening of the Chicago World's Fair in 1893 would ever forget the dazzle. Dubbed the White City for its abundance of white architecture, the fair marked the four-hundredth anniversary of Christopher Columbus's arrival in the Americas.

But the hundred thousand people who mobbed the fair's Court of Honor on May 1 were thinking more of the future than of the past. While a choir began a lively performance of George Frideric Handel's "Hallelujah Chorus," President Grover Cleveland flicked a switch that sent vast electricity-driven machines into motion. Suddenly, water gushed forth from three enormous fountains, boats rang their bells, and a cannon boomed. Fairgoers exclaimed in wonder.

By night, the fair provided an even greater spectacle. Everywhere, electric lights gleamed brightly—thousands and thousands of them. Even the fair's giant Ferris wheel glittered with three thousand bulbs. In a world where electricity was new—where many people still read by the light of gas or oil lamps and walked down pitch-black streets after dark—the sight was astounding.

"Having seen nothing but kerosene lamps for illumination, this was like getting a sudden vision of Heaven," recalled one newly arrived immigrant from Poland. Author Hamlin Garland captured the wonder when he urged his parents, "Sell the cookstove if necessary and come. You must see the fair."

In an era when electric lighting was new, the lights of the 1893 World's Fair in Chicago dazzled visitors. This photograph shows the fair's Grand Basin lit up at night.

A BITTER RIVALRY

Behind the glamour, however, and the promise of future electrical marvels, seethed a bitter dispute on the best way to distribute electricity. In some ways, the fair was the climax of that fiercely waged conflict. Fairgoers had only to visit the White City's Electricity Building to see the lines of rivalry clearly established. Facing each other at opposite ends of the vast hall, two companies, General Electric and Westinghouse Electric, vied for attention.

General Electric was a successor to the Edison Electric Light Company, founded in 1878 by U.S. inventor Thomas Edison. In the Electricity Building, people could hardly miss General Electric's display. It featured an immense lightbulb crowning an 80-foot (25-meter) tower. Five thousand sparkling pieces of glass attached to the bulb reflected its light in rainbow hues. The General Electric exhibit opened to a stirring march by composer John Philip Sousa's band while the tower was transformed into a breathtaking light show. According to the *Chicago Daily Tribune*, "Electricity danced up and down and all about [the tower] in time with the rhythm of the music." The delighted crowd broke into a spontaneous tribute to the man who had invented the first successful lightbulb. "Edison! Edison! Edison!" the people roared.

Although the Westinghouse exhibit lacked such showmanship, Westinghouse carried more weight behind the scenes. The Westinghouse Company, founded by inventor George Westinghouse, supplied the electrical equipment that powered the lights and machinery at the fair. After a long dispute with Thomas Edison about the best way to distribute electricity, Westinghouse had won the contract to power the fair.

The Westinghouse Company favored a distribution system called alternating current (or AC). Alternating current reverses direction as it travels along wires from a power plant to its destination. It moves forward and backward along the wiring many times in a second. Thomas Edison was a critic of alternating current. He said it posed too many dangers of electrical shock. Edison backed a system called direct current (or DC). In this method of delivering electricity, current travels in a straight line along electrical power lines.

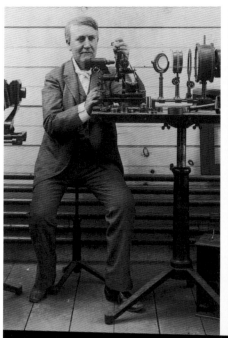

Thomas Alva Edison *(left)* and Nikola Tesla *(right)* competed fiercely over the distribution of electricity via alternating current (AC) or direct current (DC). Edison supported DC, while Tesla supported AC.

For many years, Thomas Edison did whatever he could to damage the reputation of alternating current. Meanwhile, George Westinghouse, working with inventor Nikola Tesla, argued that AC was not only safe but was also superior to direct current. By the time of the world's fair, the conflict had pretty much played itself out. But in the years leading up to 1893, competition between backers of the two systems was fierce—so fierce, in fact, that historians call it the War of the Currents.

CHAPTER 1

THOMAS EDISON:
DC CHAMPION

Before the invention of electric lighting, people spent much of their lives in semidarkness. When the sun went down, people lit their homes with candles and with lamps fueled by oil or kerosene.

Light from lamps and candles was dim, unsteady, and not well suited for reading or other close work. Nevertheless, people mended tools, wrote letters, studied, and sewed clothing by the flickering light after dark.

Lamps and candles gave off soot and smoke as they burned. Lamps had to be carefully tended and cleaned often. And if someone knocked over a candle or lamp by accident, it could easily start a fire. Each year, thousands of people died in fires involving kerosene or oil lamps.

A step up from oil and kerosene lamps was gas lighting. In the early 1800s, companies began piping gas to homes and businesses in big cities in Europe and the United States. Gas lamps provided a steadier, brighter light than lanterns. But they still had flaws. The burning gas gave off soot, which dirtied wallpaper and upholstery. The gas also gave off fumes and consumed oxygen, making the air stuffy. People often complained of headaches in homes with piped-in gas.

By the mid-1800s, electricity had started to change the way people lived and worked. Businesses and governments used the telegraph, a system for sending electrical signals along wires. The signals carried coded messages across the country and even around the world. The telephone, invented by Alexander Graham Bell in 1876, converted the human voice into electrical signals. It enabled people to talk to one another over long distances.

This photograph of a nineteenth-century tavern in London, England, shows gas lamps illuminating the area around the bar. Gas lighting was not as clean or as steady as electric lighting.

Inventors next wanted to use electricity for lighting. By the late 1870s, they had figured out how to illuminate streets and other large public spaces using electric lamps. But no one had developed a reliable, safe method of residential electric lighting. Inventor Thomas Edison wanted to be the first one to achieve that goal.

"I BELIEVE I CAN BEAT YOU"

Born in Milan, Ohio, in 1847, Thomas Edison achieved stunning success early in his career. His multiplex telegraph machine, invented in 1874, allowed telegraph operators to send more than one message at a time. His carbon sound transmitter, built in 1877, greatly improved Alexander Graham Bell's early telephone. Edison's work on this transmitter led to another great success—the invention of the phonograph, or record player.

Even with his heavy workload, Edison made time to do some preliminary experiments on electric lightbulbs. But improvements on the phonograph continued to claim most of his attention. Besides, there were "so many others working in the [electrical] field," Edison noted. He felt his talents would be better applied in other areas.

Edison's friend George Barker, a professor of physics at the University of Pennsylvania, thought differently. He believed the famous inventor could solve the problems of electric lighting better than anyone else. In 1878 Barker convinced Edison to accompany him to a brass factory in Ansonia, Connecticut. The man who owned the factory, William Wallace, had constructed the first dynamo in the United States. This machine, which turned mechanical (moving) energy into electrical energy, could be hooked up to a motor to do work. Wallace called his steam-driven dynamo a telemachon.

Wallace had also developed a way to channel the electricity generated by his dynamo into eight separate arc lamps. This kind of lamp sent a strong electric current leaping between two carbon sticks. Arc lamps gave off an intensely bright light. For several years, Wallace had been working to make arc lamps safe and efficient.

The sight of the large dynamo lighting up the lamps fascinated Edison. Back and forth he ran from the brilliant lights to the machinery that made them possible. Already his mind had forged ahead, imagining even greater possibilities. "I believe I can beat you making electric light," Edison boldly told Wallace. "I do not think you are working in the right direction." A genial handshake between the two men sealed their competition.

> "I believe I can beat you making electric light. I do not think you are working in the right direction."
>
> Thomas Edison to dynamo maker
> William Wallace, 1878

INCANDESCENCE

For Edison, the right direction had nothing to do with arc lamps that sent light leaping across space. He wanted to devise a lighting system based on incandescence. In such a system, the electricity passing through a substance

ARC LAMPS— THE DOWNSIDE

In the 1880s, many cities in Europe and the United States used arc lamps to light streets, parks, and other public places. Some large businesses also installed arc lighting. But despite the growing interest, arc lamps had serious problems. They produced a lot of smoke, and the carbon sticks that carried the lamps' electric current had to be adjusted frequently as they burned. In addition, arc lights were intensely bright, almost blinding. For this reason, they were better suited for outdoor illumination and for large spaces such as factories than for use in homes.

heats it up so much that it begins to glow. The principle is simple, but the job itself was fraught with difficulty. Although other inventors had already managed to create incandescent light, no one had yet developed a lamp or lightbulb that was long lasting and reliable.

Edison decided to use trial and error to discover the right filament—the thin, threadlike substance inside an incandescent lamp that glows when heated. At Edison's research workshop in Menlo Park, New Jersey, he and his colleagues tested more than sixteen hundred different kinds of filaments. One type of cotton thread proved promising. It burned for forty hours. But Edison wasn't satisfied. Eventually, he and his crew created a bamboo filament that burned for twelve hundred hours—thirty times longer!

By this time, several electric companies were selling arc lighting systems to New York City businesses. The electric companies strung overhead wires, which carried electric current to hotels, theaters, and many other public places. Mingling with telephone and telegraph lines, the wires formed an unsightly maze over the streets.

Edison also wanted to electrify New York—but with incandescent lighting and with underground electrical wires. To do this, he needed more than just bulbs. "I have to make the dynamos, the lamps, the conductors [wires], and attend to a thousand details the world never hears of," Edison declared. No one person could do it all. Relying heavily on his growing staff, Edison supervised the experiments and research.

Experiment No. 1. Feby 13 1880

small horseshoe

In 1880 Thomas Edison made this sketch of an incandescent lightbulb in his notebook. The sketch shows a filament inside a glass bulb.

JUMBOS

In 1881 Edison bought two buildings on Pearl Street in New York City, where he planned to build his first electrical power station. The buildings were not far from the city's financial center, Wall Street. This location would give Edison the opportunity to light up the offices of some of the wealthiest men in the nation. First, he would need dynamos (also called generators) bigger than any in existence. He created 7-ton (6.4-metric-ton) dynamos he dubbed jumbos and put six of them into the Pearl Street plant. Edison later recalled, "The engines and dynamos made a horrible racket from loud and deep groans to a hideous shriek, and the place seemed to be filled with sparks and flames of all colors."

Edison poses with one of his jumbo dynamos. Dynamos, also called generators, convert mechanical energy into electrical energy.

Like other dynamos, Edison's noisy machines first turned out an alternating current. Devices called commutators then collected the electrical charge and changed it to direct current. The electricity traveled along underground wires to homes and businesses.

"I HAVE ACCOMPLISHED ALL I PROMISED"

"The Pearl Street Station was the biggest and most responsible thing I had ever undertaken," Edison would later remember. "What might happen on

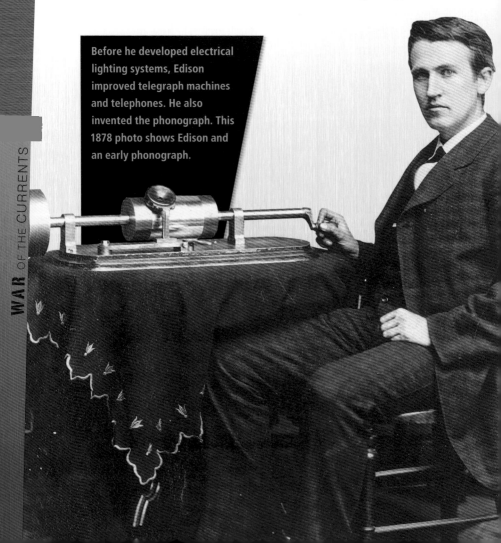

Before he developed electrical lighting systems, Edison improved telegraph machines and telephones. He also invented the phonograph. This 1878 photo shows Edison and an early phonograph.

turning a big current into the conductors under the streets of New York no one could say."

The time to find out came on September 4, 1882. By then Edison had formed the Edison Electric Light Company. He and members of his board of directors assembled in the Wall Street office of board member and banker J. P. Morgan while they waited for a switch to be thrown in the Pearl Street Station. If all went well, the incandescent lamps in the office would start to glow.

"One hundred dollars they don't go on," board member Edward Johnson bet Edison as the moment drew near.

"Taken!" cried Edison.

To the relief and delight of everyone present, the lamps lit up. Even Johnson was happy to lose his bet. "I have accomplished all I promised," Edison told a newspaper reporter.

> ## "One hundred dollars they don't go on."
>
> Edward Johnson, board member of the Edison Electric Light Company, waiting for lamps to light up, September 4, 1882

Four months later, his power station was providing electricity to 231 customers with more than thirty-four hundred lamps. After almost a year, 431 houses (and ten thousand lamps) depended on the Pearl Street Station for power. By 1884 Edison's company was running central power plants in Boston, Massachusetts; Chicago, Illinois; New Orleans, Louisiana; and other U.S. cities. Eager to build on his accomplishments, Edison hoped to spread his DC lighting system all over the world.

CHAPTER 2

NIKOLA TESLA: THE CHALLENGE OF AC

In the 1860s, in a little town in Croatia (then part of Austria–Hungary), a boy named Nikola Tesla was fascinated by electricity. He read everything he could find on the subject, and he experimented with batteries and other electrical devices.

One day young Tesla saw a picture of Niagara Falls, an enormous waterfall between Canada and the United States. Immediately he visualized a giant waterwheel converting the energy of the waterfall into electrical power. Someday, he told his uncle, he would go to the United States to carry out his plan.

Years later, in 1875, Tesla entered the Joanneum Polytechnic School in Graz, Austria. There, in physics class, a demonstration further piqued his interest in electricity. Professor Jacob Poeschl had brought a dynamo to class. Watching the dynamo perform, Tesla thought it was needlessly complicated.

Like all dynamos of this era, the one Poeschl demonstrated produced alternating current and then converted it to direct current with commutators. But commutators were not high-quality machines. They wore out quickly and often posed hazards. In fact, as Poeschl demonstrated the dynamo to his class that day, its commutators sparked dangerously.

Tesla thought that the machine would run more smoothly if the commutators were eliminated. Then he began to wonder why alternating current had to be changed to direct current at all. Surely a system could be devised whereby alternating current could be used to power machinery, he thought.

When Tesla voiced his opinion, however, the teacher was scornful. Poeschl spent the rest of the class explaining why Tesla's idea would not work. According to the professor, it was simply not possible to efficiently harness alternating current. "Mr. Tesla may do many things," he declared, "but this he can not accomplish."

As a boy in Croatia, Nikola Tesla saw a picture of Niagara Falls *(below)*. He envisioned using the rushing water to turn giant spinning blades to create electricity.

Tesla felt humiliated by the stinging criticism. But in the end, Poeschl's arguments failed to sway him. In his heart, Tesla believed he could do what the professor said was impossible. He could make a system for powering machines with alternating current.

Other engineers had been thinking along similar lines. In the United States, inventor Elihu Thomson had built a generator to power arc lights with alternating current. With Thomson's system and others like it, power fluctuated as the alternating current changed direction as it traveled along electrical wires. This system was fine for powering arc lights, which had no moving parts. But motors needed continuous power that did not fluctuate. Tesla determined to figure out how to solve this problem.

"A SACRED VOW"

Tesla never graduated from the Joanneum Polytechnic School, partly because he didn't have enough money. Eventually he took a job at a telephone company in Budapest, Hungary. In his spare time, he continued to seek a practical way

VOLTAGE

The force that causes electric current to flow, voltage, is measured in units called volts. To get an idea of voltage, imagine blowing gently through a straw. Then visualize sending all the breath you can muster through the straw. The force of the air moving through the straw has increased. Then imagine an electric current moving either gently or forcefully along wire. The gentle current has a lower voltage than the forceful current. Voltage tells us the force of a current, but it does not tell us the *amount* of current passing through a wire. The amount of current is measured in a unit called amperes, or amps.

to deliver alternating current to homes and businesses. The answer seemed tantalizingly close yet remained just out of reach. "With me it was a sacred vow," said Tesla, "a question of life or death. I knew I would perish if I failed."

One afternoon Tesla walked through a park in Budapest with a good friend, Anthony Szigety. The setting sun brought a passage from a favorite German play to Tesla's mind. As he pronounced the words, the answer he had been seeking arrived "like a flash of lightning." Dropping to the ground, he snatched a twig and began to draw a diagram in the dirt.

Rapidly, Tesla outlined a way to use two alternating currents inside a motor. A current consists of electrically charged particles flowing along a wire. Inside a motor, a current creates a magnetic field, which is pulled on by other magnets in the motor. This pull causes the magnetic field to spin. The spinning magnetic field turns the shaft of the motor. DC motors needed commutators to spin the magnetic field. In Tesla's motor, the magnetic field spun without commutators. And the two electric currents kept the motor spinning at full strength, with no gaps in which the power of the motor weakened.

Inside an AC Motor

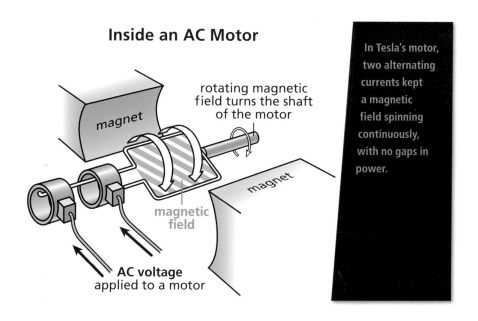

rotating magnetic field turns the shaft of the motor

magnet

magnetic field

magnet

AC voltage applied to a motor

In Tesla's motor, two alternating currents kept a magnetic field spinning continuously, with no gaps in power.

For weeks Tesla devoted himself to working out the details for all sorts of AC machinery. His creativity poured forth in such a torrent of ideas that he could scarcely keep up with them. In his imagination, he saw his motors in continual operation. In less than two months, Tesla worked out all the details for a new system to generate and distribute alternating current.

Without money and resources, Tesla faced an uphill battle to get his system put into use. Then, in 1882, the U.S.-based Edison Electric Light Company offered him a job in its office in Paris, France. Tesla saw this position as an opportunity to interest people at the forefront of the electrical revolution in his ideas. In addition to his native Croatian, he spoke French, German, and English, so working abroad did not pose a problem. He accepted the offer. However, once in Paris, he was discouraged to learn that Thomas Edison was already an outspoken critic of alternating current.

Despite this setback to his hopes, Tesla had an interesting job and an exciting city to explore. His job performance proved outstanding. Impressed, Tesla's manager, Charles Batchelor, encouraged him to go to the United States, where he might be able to work with Edison himself. Tesla needed little persuasion to embark on what promised to be a great adventure.

The day after his ship docked in New York, Tesla visited Edison at his lab. Neither man would ever forget the meeting. Edison, short and solidly built, dressed simply and spoke bluntly. In contrast, Tesla dressed formally. Manners and poise meant a great deal to him. Despite their differences, the two men sensed a common bond. Pleased with Tesla's knowledge and accomplishments, Edison hired the newcomer.

After several weeks, Edison gave Tesla his first major challenge. Edison's company had installed a lighting system on a passenger ship, the USS *Oregon*. However, the dynamos that supplied the vessel's electricity had broken. Tesla spent an entire night working with crew members to locate and repair short circuits. His quick and reliable work earned praise from Edison. "This is a good man," he muttered.

In addition to repair work, Edison asked Tesla to redesign some important pieces of equipment. Heedless of sleep, Tesla worked regularly from ten

Thomas Edison *(circled)* poses with his assistants at his laboratory in Menlo Park, New Jersey, in the 1870s. The lab eventually expanded to fill two city blocks.

thirty in the morning, through the day and night, until five the next morning. "I have had many hard working assistants," Edison told him, "but you take the cake."

> "I have had many hard working assistants, but you take the cake."
>
> Thomas Edison to Nikola Tesla, 1884

AC VERSUS DC

"All the time," Tesla wrote later, "I was getting more and more anxious about the invention [the AC motor] and was making up my mind to place it before Edison." He hoped to persuade his employer that alternating current was not only safe but also more practical and economical than direct current.

The DC system used by Edison was a low-voltage system. Voltage is a force that causes electric current to flow. Edison preferred a low-voltage system because he thought it was safer than a high-voltage system. Edison noted that a person who touched any part of his electrical equipment would receive no more than a mild shock. To further ensure safety, Edison buried his lines underground rather than stringing them overhead.

Edison's DC system had one big disadvantage, however. In Edison's low-voltage system, electricity could be transmitted efficiently and economically for only about 1 mile (1.6 kilometers). This made the system practical for lighting a large home or a group of nearby buildings, such as Wall Street's financial district, but not for lighting streets and neighborhoods running for many miles through a city.

Alternating current, on the other hand, traveled at much higher voltages and had the force to travel much greater distances. One AC power station could deliver electricity to a large area, thereby keeping expenses down. Edison acknowledged this advantage, but he argued that AC's high voltage posed a great risk of shock and even death to those who accidentally came into contact with it.

PARTING OF THE WAYS

Tesla never persuaded Edison to give alternating current a chance. "Spare me that nonsense," Edison replied when Tesla broached the subject. "[AC] is dangerous. We're set up for direct current in America. People like it, and it's all I'll ever fool with."

Tesla's employer could be remarkably stubborn in other ways too, as Tesla learned in a dispute over money. A company manager had promised Tesla a $50,000 bonus for improving twenty-four machines. But Tesla received no payment when the task was complete. In dismay, he approached his boss. Edison laughed. How could Tesla have expected such an enormous sum? After all, his regular salary was only $18 a week. "When you become a full-fledged American, you will appreciate an American joke," Edison said.

> "[AC] is dangerous. We're set up for direct current in America. People like it, and it's all I'll ever fool with."
>
> Thomas Edison, circa 1885

Tesla saw nothing funny in the situation. Feeling cheated and hurt, he resigned.

Soon after leaving the Edison Electric Light Company, Tesla thought his moment for worldly success had finally come. While filing for patents (government documents awarding him the rights to make and sell his inventions and prohibiting others from doing so), he met two businessmen who professed an interest in his AC motor. Tesla agreed to form a company with them.

His first task with the firm was to install and improve a system of AC-powered arc lighting for a small town. He thought the company would then expand into AC motors. After a year, however, his partners found a way to take complete control of the business. They never had any intention of developing Tesla's AC inventions. A shocked Tesla later described the situation as "the hardest blow I ever received."

TESLA ELECTRIC COMPANY

Bitter and broke, Tesla took a job digging ditches. But his work in arc lighting had brought him some favorable publicity, and eventually Tesla interested some investors in his ideas for alternating current. With this money, he founded the Tesla Electric Light Company. By April 1887, he had opened a laboratory and workshops on South Fifth Street in New York.

Eager to succeed, Tesla worked almost continuously. In a burst of feverish activity, he developed three distinct systems for generating and distributing alternating current: single-phase, double-phase, and polyphase.

Other inventors already used single-phase AC systems to power arc lighting. To power motors, Tesla perfected the system he had envisioned in Hungary on his walk with Anthony Szigety. In this setup, multiple pulses of current traveled along different sets of wires, powering a motor at full strength. In a two-phase system, two currents were out of sync, so as one current diminished, the other current increased. Polyphase systems consisted of three or more out-of-sync alternating currents. These currents delivered full power to a motor almost continuously.

A complete system for alternating current also required its own dynamos, motors, and other devices. Tesla invented all the necessary machines for each of his three systems. He created transformers, which boosted the voltage produced by a dynamo. The increase in voltage allowed electricity to travel longer distances over wires. Before the current entered homes or businesses,

WAR OF THE CURRENTS

Direct current moves in a straight line. Alternating current reverses direction as it travels. In this diagram, where the alternating current peaks above and below the 0 line, the greatest amount of current is flowing. Where the alternating current crosses the 0 line, no power is flowing. By using two (or more) currents out of sync with each other (two-phase AC), Tesla minimized gaps in the flow.

Three Types of Current

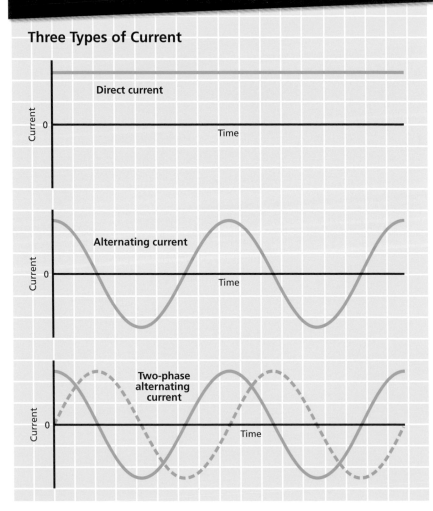

ROW, ROW, ROW

To better understand polyphase AC, imagine people singing "Row, row, row your boat." One person singing would be like a single cycle of AC. Four people singing in a round would be like four-phase AC. With four people singing, the sound would be uninterrupted.

another transformer reduced the voltage. This was an important safety factor. It was also another advantage of AC over DC, which couldn't be stepped up and down with transformers.

As Tesla's first AC motors went into production, he began to attract more attention. Soon Thomas Martin, editor of the respected journal *Electrical World*, paid Tesla a visit and talked him into writing an article for publication.

About a year after Tesla's company was formed, Martin convinced him to give a talk at the newly established American Institute of Electrical Engineers (AIEE). Whether it was the depth of his knowledge, his passion for the subject, or a combination of both, Tesla proved to be a dynamic speaker. Electricians all over the world took note of his lecture and the exciting possibility of AC motors.

CHAPTER 3

ENTER GEORGE
WESTINGHOUSE

Nikola Tesla was not the only person to note the advantages of alternating current. Inventor and businessman George Westinghouse also believed that the future belonged to AC.

For many years, Westinghouse worked in the railroad business. In 1885 he bought a gas company and began piping gas to light homes in Pittsburgh, Pennsylvania.

Westinghouse was intrigued by electricity. He had visited Edison's workshop in Menlo Park, witnessed the stunning success of the lightbulb, and received a warm welcome from the inventor. But he realized the limits of direct current. He knew that since DC could be transmitted only about 1 mile (1.6 km) from its source, many power stations would have to be built as more and more homes and businesses wanted electric power.

Westinghouse wanted to get in on the ground floor of the alternating current business. Two engineers, Lucien Gaulard of France and John Gibbs of Britain, had developed a transformer for decreasing the high voltage of alternating current before it entered homes. Westinghouse bought the rights to distribute the transformer in the United States. As part of the deal, Gaulard and Gibbs sent several transformers and an AC generator to the Westinghouse headquarters in Pittsburgh.

In the late 1800s, George Westinghouse provided power to homes and businesses using alternating current. He started his career in the railroad business, inventing air brakes for trains in the 1860s.

Excitement soon turned to disappointment. Initial tests of the transformer showed that it didn't control voltage well and was prone to breakdowns. Westinghouse assigned William Stanley, one of his best engineers, the task of improving the transformer. Working together, Stanley and Westinghouse redesigned the device.

TESTING THE TRANSFORMER

Stanley and Westinghouse planned to offer an AC lighting system in Stanley's hometown of Great Barrington, Massachusetts. Working in secret so his competitors wouldn't find out, Stanley put six improved transformers in the basements of buildings that had signed up for the new AC system.

As it turned out, Thomas Edison beat George Westinghouse in demonstrating electric light in the small town. A wealthy Great Barrington resident wanted Edison to install a small power plant in his home. In early March 1886, the home's new electric lights blazed forth for all to see. Returning from a well-deserved vacation, Stanley was mightily annoyed.

One week later, Stanley was ready for his own test run. He sent 500 volts of electricity along copper wires to the basement of his cousin's store, where a transformer lowered the electricity to 100 volts. Wires from the transformer led to incandescent lightbulbs upstairs. Within seconds, the dusky shop was aglow. "Two of the lights in the store made it as light as noon-day," reported a local paper.

RIVALRY BEGINS

Stanley continued to tie more buildings into the system. Finally, all was ready for the grand debut of the Westinghouse AC system in Great Barrington. On March 30, 1886, hundreds of townsfolk lined the streets to witness the display. As darkness fell, thirteen buildings lit up.

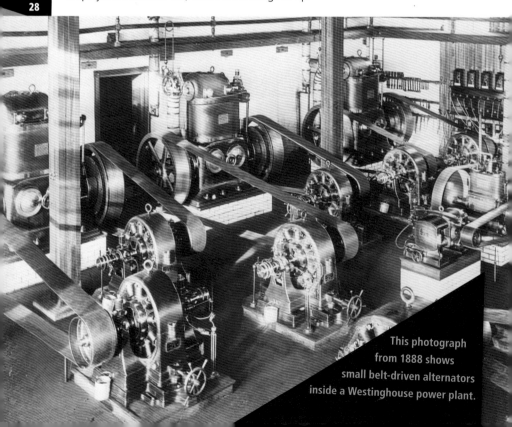

This photograph from 1888 shows small belt-driven alternators inside a Westinghouse power plant.

In short order, Stanley lined up dozens of other customers. The Edison Electric Light Company could not compete with him. Its inability to send DC power long distances posed a serious handicap.

Elated with his success, Westinghouse ran more tests on his AC system. Around Thanksgiving 1886, he opened his first commercial AC power plant in Buffalo, New York. Other communities took note of the Westinghouse success in Buffalo. Soon the company had contracts to build twenty-seven more AC stations. The growth of the rival business angered Thomas Edison. "I don't much care for fortune," he once said, "as I do for getting ahead of the other fellow."

> "I don't much care for fortune . . . as I do for getting ahead of the other fellow."
>
> Thomas Edison, n.d.

Edison tried to stay ahead of Westinghouse by bringing lawsuits against him for infringing on, or violating, his patents. He charged his rival with copying the design of his incandescent lamps. "It is all bunkum [nonsense] on their part," Westinghouse retorted in an interview with the *Pittsburgh Dispatch*. "We have patents on our systems of incandescent lights that are so immeasurably superior to theirs it is only a question of time before we supersede them [take over their business] all over the country."

Although the Westinghouse Electric Company continued to grow, AC systems still lacked a

> "It is all bunkum on their [Edison's] part. We have patents on our system of incandescent lights that are so immeasurably superior to theirs it is only a question of time before we supersede them [take over their business] all over the country."
>
> George Westinghouse, December 1887 or early 1888

motor that would run efficiently. All the electric motors then in use could run on only direct current. Alternating current could be used only to power lights, not to run machinery.

Then Nikola Tesla came to George Westinghouse's attention. Just days after Tesla's successful lecture at the AIEE, Westinghouse contacted him. He knew that Tesla had the missing piece needed to make AC available for all electrical uses. He also knew that Tesla had filed patents for his motors and for other parts of his AC system. If Westinghouse wanted to use AC to power machinery, he needed Nikola Tesla.

Tesla liked Westinghouse almost at once. He realized that Westinghouse was a man who did not back down from a fight. Tesla also knew that sooner or later, a showdown with Thomas Edison was inevitable. Telsa wanted Westinghouse as his ally in that showdown. The two men rapidly came to an agreement. As part of the arrangement, Tesla moved to Pittsburgh to work with Westinghouse.

THE GRANDEST INVENTION

After AC lighting came to Buffalo in 1886, a department store named Adam, Meldrum & Anderson advertised its new lighting system proudly: "The appearance is brilliant in the extreme. The light is steady and colorless. Shades [of clothing and other fabrics for sale] can be perfectly matched. Come and see the grandest invention of the nineteenth century."

"AS CERTAIN AS DEATH"

The association between Westinghouse and Tesla added fuel to Edison's already considerable anger. As long as Westinghouse lacked an AC motor, Edison had a crucial competitive edge. But somewhere down the road, if Westinghouse could offer more than lighting to his customers, Edison would face a serious threat to his business. Once alternating current could power such devices as mining equipment, welding tools, trolleys, stoves, heaters, and clothes washing machines, DC would have lost a major advantage.

In his bitterness, Edison made a dire prediction: "Just as certain as death Westinghouse will kill a customer [via accidental electrocution] within six months after he puts in a system of any size. He has got a new thing and it will require a great deal of experimenting to get it working practically. It will never be free from danger." The battle lines had been clearly drawn. Edison was ready to declare war.

CHAPTER 4

RIVALRY

BECOMES WAR

While the Edison and Westinghouse companies competed for customers and argued about safety, the state of New York was considering another use for electricity.

Public sentiment had been growing against the practice of executing criminals by hanging. If the executioner didn't use just the right length of rope, a person who died by hanging might either suffocate slowly or even be beheaded by the noose. If someone was sentenced to die, reasoned lawmakers, surely there was a more humane method of execution.

New York lawmakers created a commission to investigate the options. It conducted a survey of legal and medical professionals. On the basis of responses, the commission concluded that most people thought electrocution was more humane than hanging.

On November 8, 1887, Dr. Alfred Southwick, a Buffalo dentist who served on the commission, wrote to Thomas Edison for advice. He wanted to know how strong a current had to be to ensure a speedy death by electrocution. He also asked for Edison's idea as to the cost of constructing a suitable apparatus.

Thomas Edison was appalled. He did not support the death penalty and had no intention of helping the commission. In his reply, he said that the threat of life imprisonment did as much to halt would-be murderers as fear of the death penalty. He wanted nothing to do with killing anyone.

Southwick wrote back, arguing that the death penalty was a reality and most likely would continue to be. The commission couldn't change that, but it could propose a more civilized and pain-free method of execution. Southwick added that the members would be especially receptive to whatever advice Edison had to offer.

EDISON'S TURNABOUT

A month after the first letter, Edison was feeling differently. Although he still opposed the death penalty, he saw an opportunity to gain ground in his ongoing battle against alternating current. In a complete about-face, Edison wrote back that if a prisoner were condemned to die by electricity, alternating current should be used. He even mentioned his rival by name. "The most suitable apparatus for the purpose [execution]," he wrote, "is that class of dynamo-electric machines which employs intermittent currents [AC]. The most effective of these are known

> "The most suitable apparatus for the purpose [execution] is that class of dynamo—electric machines which employs intermittent currents. The most effective of these are known as 'alternating currents' manufactured in this country by George Westinghouse."
>
> Thomas Edison, December 1888

as 'alternating machines,' manufactured principally in this country by George Westinghouse. . . . The passage of current from these machines through the human body, even by the slightest contacts, produces instantaneous death."

Edison believed everything he wrote. But he also hoped that if people associated alternating current with electrocution, they would think twice before allowing it in their homes or workplaces.

As far as Edison was concerned, it was impossible to overestimate the dangers of alternating current. In his effort to sway public opinion, in February 1888 he published a brochure in boldly titled, "A WARNING FROM THE EDISON ELECTRIC LIGHT COMPANY." The pamphlet described several accidents in which people had died from coming in contact with AC wires. Calling the Edison record "glorious," the brochure stressed that "there has never been a single instance of loss of life from the current employed [DC]."

ELECTRICAL TRAGEDIES

Edison's warning was well timed. As outdoor arc lighting came into more general use and more electrical wires hung in tangles above city streets, accidents were bound to occur. Sometimes storms damaged the wires. Sometimes businesses neglected to take down frayed

This photograph from the late 1800s shows a maze of electrical and telephone lines above the streets of New York City. Someone who touched a fallen power line could be electrocuted.

or loose wires. A tragedy occurred on April 15, 1888, when a fifteen-year-old New York City boy named Moses Streiffer unthinkingly grabbed a broken telegraph wire drooping from a pole. In a lighthearted mood, he began to prance around the pole. Suddenly sparks crackled in the air. Moses tottered and crumbled on the sidewalk. An ambulance rushed him to the hospital, where he was pronounced dead.

The next person to die was an employee of the Brush Electric Company who was electrocuted while clearing out old wires from the second story of a building, also in New York City. Rescue workers received swift shocks as they tried to retrieve the body. The two senseless deaths, less than a month apart, alarmed the public. Newspapers took up the crusade against the dangers posed by the growing jumble of exposed electric wires. Citizens called for electric companies to follow the example of Thomas Edison in placing wires underground.

On June 5, 1888, a new voice joined the fray to fight for electrical safety. Spurred by the recent tragedies, electrical engineer Harold P. Brown published a long, hostile letter, titled "Death in the Wires," in the *New York Evening Post*. Brown contended that underground wires, while important, were not enough to prevent accidents. Brown urged the New York City Board of Electrical Control to prohibit the use of alternating current over 300 volts. The board members took Brown's letter very seriously when it was read aloud at their next meeting. The board sent copies of the letter to the different electric light companies in the city, as well as to George Westinghouse.

"A GREAT DEAL OF MISCHIEF"

Around the time Brown was attacking alternating current, George Westinghouse was welcoming Nikola Tesla to Pittsburgh to begin work on his AC motor. It was a time of optimism and excitement for both men. Neither took Brown's ravings seriously. Both knew that properly used, alternating current was as safe as direct current. Saddened by the increasingly bitter controversy, Westinghouse saw no need for such ill will. He wrote an honest and friendly letter to Thomas Edison.

In this Westinghouse lab, Nikola Tesla worked to perfect his AC motor.

No doubt with Brown in mind, Westinghouse noted, "I believe there has been a systematic attempt on the part of some people to do a great deal of mischief and create as great a difference as possible between the Edison Company and The Westinghouse Electric Co., when there ought to be an entirely different condition of affairs." Recalling past meetings with Edison, one at Menlo Park, Westinghouse invited his rival to visit him in Pittsburgh.

Edison's reply was short and somewhat brusque. "My laboratory work consumes the whole of my time. . . . Thanking you for your kind invitation to visit you in Pittsburgh." The peace offering had been firmly refused.

Westinghouse never renewed his goodwill advances. After learning that Edison's sales force had accused his own company of lying, the beleaguered Westinghouse struck back with a forceful letter to the New York City Board of Electrical Control. He defended his company vigorously and accused his competitors of a "method of attack which has been more unmanly, discreditable and untruthful than any competition which has ever come to my knowledge."

The debate between supporters of AC and DC raged on. At the next meeting of the New York City Board of Electrical Control, several electricians spoke scornfully of Harold Brown's conclusions. Brown, who had been out of town at the time of the meeting, was angry and determined to fight back.

Hoping to enlist the support of Thomas Edison, Brown paid an unexpected call on the world-famous inventor. He wanted to discuss a rather gruesome demonstration he had in mind. "To my surprise," Brown later recalled, "Mr. Edison at once invited me to make the experiments at his private laboratory, and placed all necessary apparatus at my disposal." Unknown to the press and public until several years later, Brown began to work closely with Edison and the Thomson-Houston Company, another competitor of Westinghouse.

> "[My opponents have used a] method of attack which has been more unmanly, discreditable and untruthful than any competition which has ever come to my knowledge."
>
> George Westinghouse, July 14, 1888

Brown set up a dynamo that could generate up to 1,500 volts and proceeded to subject stray dogs to varying voltages of both alternating and direct current. He wanted to determine what level of voltage was required to kill. Eventually he determined that dogs could withstand more than 1,000 volts of direct current. A mere 300 volts of alternating current, however, would cause immediate death.

Satisfied that he had proved his point, Brown arranged for a public demonstration. On July 30, 1888, members of the New York City's electrical board, officials from various electric light companies, and reporters gathered in a lecture room at Columbia College. Brown led a 76-pound (34-kilogram) black retriever onto the stage and shocked him repeatedly. Although the dog withstood 1,000 volts of DC, he died when 330 volts of AC went coursing through his body.

Did this demonstration prove that alternating current was more deadly than direct current? Brown believed that it did, but AC supporters in the audience objected angrily. The dog had already been greatly weakened from consecutive surges of direct current, they noted. In his former healthy state, he might well have survived the burst of alternating current.

Ready for their arguments, Brown then proposed to kill a second dog solely with alternating current. But his audience had had enough. A reporter for the *New York World* cried out for an end to Brown's "inhuman performance." Seconding his protest, a man climbed onstage and showed a badge, revealing himself as superintendent of the Society for the Prevention of Cruelty to Animals. He called an immediate halt to the proceedings.

But Brown was not to be deterred for long. Several days later, he demonstrated another round of experiments on dogs. He felt confident that his results would influence state lawmakers. "It is certain that yesterday's work will get a law passed by the legislature in the fall, limiting the Voltage of alternating currents to 300 Volts," he wrote to a colleague of Edison's. Such a law would eliminate AC's practical advantage over DC. If AC could not be transmitted at high voltages, it would not be able to travel long distances from a power station to its destination.

THE EXECUTIONER'S CURRENT

On June 4, 1888, the day before Brown's angry letter had been published in the *New York Evening Post*, New York governor David Hill had signed an electrical execution bill, which authorized the killing of condemned prisoners by electric chair.

Effective as of January 1, 1889, the bill left many technical details to be worked out by a respected New York organization, the Medico-Legal Society. These issues included the question of whether direct or alternating current would be used in putting a prisoner to death. Dr. Frederick Peterson, who had helped Brown electrocute animals at Columbia College, was put in charge of a committee to investigate which type of current should be used. Basing their decision on more tests done by Brown, the committee selected alternating current.

George Westinghouse was quick to respond to the society's decision. Although he was infuriated, he managed to keep his rage in check and present his views matter-of-factly in a newspaper advertisement. He stressed the safety of alternating current and claimed that Thomas Edison had supported and financed Harold Brown's experiments. Such backing, of course, compromised Brown's objectivity. "The [AC] business," Westinghouse declared, "would not have had . . . enormous and rapid growth if it had been as dangerous as its opponents charged."

Brown wasted little time in countering Westinghouse's charges with some scathing accusations of his own. Brown sent letters to mayors, city council members, and businesspeople in every U.S. town with a population over five thousand. Referring to AC as the new "executioner's current," he urged everyone to "protect the lives of those dear to you" by resisting the spread of alternating current.

In March 1889, two months after the electric execution law went into effect, New York State prison officials asked Harold Brown to provide and install the equipment needed for an execution. Here was another opportunity to slam Thomas Edison's opponent. Although several companies manufactured AC generators, Brown decided that only Westinghouse generators should be used to execute prisoners. Of course, he knew that George Westinghouse would never sell him a generator. Resorting to trickery, he had generators purchased through a third party.

"THE WIZARD TESTIFIES"

As Brown was making preparations for the delivery of a generator to New York's Auburn State Prison, a man named William Kemmler was being tried for murder. Convicted of killing his girlfriend in a drunken rage, he was sentenced to die.

The U.S. Constitution forbade punishment that was deemed "cruel and unusual." Kemmler's attorney, W. Bourke Cockran, believed that electrocution fell into this category. He filed an appeal, in which he contended that Brown's animal experiments were no guarantee that a human would die quickly and painlessly by electricity. He cited a case in which a dog had brushed against a broken telegraph wire and seemingly been killed by electricity, only to revive several hours later. Cockran contended that what had happened to a dog could happen to a man. If William Kemmler revived after initial application of electricity, would he be subject to a second dose? Such a fate could clearly be considered cruel and unusual, Cockran said.

During the appeal, Thomas Edison was called in to testify. "In your judgment, can artificial electric current be generated and applied in such a way to produce death in human beings in every case?" demanded Cockran.

"Yes," replied Edison.

"Instantly?" pressed Cockran.

"Yes," said Edison again.

Newspapers headlined his testimony, declaring in bold letters:

EDISON SAYS IT WILL KILL, THE WIZARD TESTIFIES AS AN EXPERT IN THE KEMMLER CASE, HE THINKS AN ARTIFICIAL CURRENT CAN BE GENERATED WHICH WILL PRODUCE DEATH INSTANTLY AND PAINLESSLY IN EVERY CASE—ONE THOUSAND VOLTS OF AN ALTERNATING CURRENT WOULD BE SUFFICIENT.

Auburn State Prison in New York was the site of William Kemmler's execution by alternating current in 1890.

On October 12, 1889, Judge Edwin Day upheld Kemmler's sentence. Immediately Cockran appealed to the New York Supreme Court. After that court rejected his appeal, Cockran took his client's case all the way to the U.S. Supreme Court. In early August 1890, the Supreme Court ruled that New York's decision should stand.

Thomas Edison's forces relished the victory. Someone even suggested that Westinghouse's name be given to the electric chair. Instead of a prisoner being electrocuted, a condemned man would be "westinghoused."

A BUNGLED EXECUTION

A crowd gathered outside the prison on August 6, the day William Kemmler was to be executed. Before he was strapped into the electric chair, Kemmler expressed willingness to die for his crime. "Now take your time and do it right," he told the warden. "I don't want to take any chances on this thing [the chair not working], you know."

This illustration, published in *Scientific American* magazine in June 1888, shows execution by electrocution.

A MAN BURSTING
WITH IDEAS

As much as he admired George Westinghouse, Nikola Tesla felt hampered by the restrictions placed upon him at the Westinghouse Company in Pittsburgh. He returned to New York in late 1889 and opened his own laboratory.

Always teeming with ideas, Tesla worked on many projects. To create very high-voltage currents, he built machines called oscillators, later known as Tesla coils *(right)*. He experimented with gas in glass tubes to create bright neon light. Radio waves also fascinated him. He built and tested both radio transmitters and receivers. In addition, he constructed automatons, robotic machines controlled by radio waves. After the discovery of X-rays in 1895, Tesla made a number of X-ray images (which he called shadowgraphs) of his own body and others' bodies.

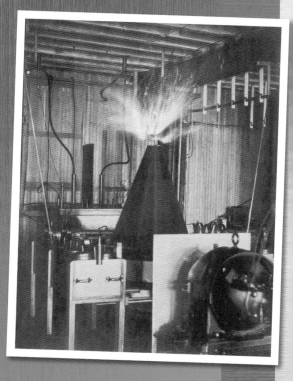

But the chair didn't work correctly. Kemmler was mistakenly pronounced dead and removed from the chair while his heart was still beating. He had to be strapped into the chair and electrocuted a second time. The second surge of electricity burned his skin and hair. Witnesses to the execution were emotionally shaken. Some nearly vomited. "FAR WORSE THAN HANGING," proclaimed the *New York Times* in front-page headlines.

George Westinghouse believed that the botched job proved that alternating current was not as deadly as his opponents had charged, but Kemmler's death still sent ripples of alarm through the public. Even President Benjamin Harrison and his wife were said to be afraid to touch the switches of an AC lighting system installed in the White House.

Despite the initial setback, the execution did not hurt Westinghouse sales as Edison hoped it would. Soon Baltimore, Maryland; Elmira, New York; and Lincoln, Nebraska, ordered AC light systems. One year after Kemmler's death, Westinghouse had cornered more than half the lighting market.

ON THE SIDELINES

During the War of the Currents and the terrible controversy surrounding Kemmler's electrocution, Nikola Tesla remained on the sidelines. He was not a fighter. He was convinced that alternating current would ultimately triumph, but he left George Westinghouse to counter the accusations of Thomas Edison's forces. He hailed Westinghouse as "the only man on this globe who could take my alternating system under the circumstances then existing and win the battle against prejudice and money power. He was a pioneer of imposing stature, one of the world's noblemen."

CHAPTER 5

WATER AND LIGHT

Many years had passed since Nikola Tesla had imagined Niagara Falls generating electricity. Other people were beginning to see the possibility too.

In the late 1880s, a group of investors formed the Niagara Falls Power Company. Its goal was to convert the rushing energy of the waterfall into electrical current.

GROUNDBREAKING

On October 4, 1890, even before a precise plan was formalized, a groundbreaking ceremony was held for construction of a huge tunnel. The tunnel would carry rushing water from the falls to machines called turbines, which look like giant propellers. The force of the rushing water would spin the turbines to generate electricity. More than thirteen hundred men would dig the tunnel with sledgehammers, steam shovels, and dynamite.

Tesla conducted spectacular demonstrations of electricity. In this image, published in the *Electrical Review* in 1899, Tesla safely surrounds his body with electrical charges.

Meanwhile, a group of five men known as the International Niagara Commission sought proposals from electric companies for the best scheme to harness the falls. William Thomson of Britain, who headed the commission, was an outspoken critic of alternating current. Most of the other members agreed with him, even though AC was forging ahead of DC commercially. The commission wanted electricity from the falls to be used for more than lighting, but at that time, Nikola Tesla's AC motor still hadn't proved itself. The commissioners didn't yet know whether alternating current could be used to power machinery.

"Avoid the gigantic error of alternating current."

William Thomson, in a message to the International Niagara Commission, May 1893

THE CASE FOR AC

Several things happened to change the commissioners' minds. In 1891 a generator sent 3,000 volts of alternating current 3 miles (4.8 km) up a mountainside to the Gold King Mine in Telluride, Colorado. There, AC motors designed by Tesla powered machinery that crushed ore, showing that alternating current was practical for more than just lighting. Statistics also showed that AC was satisfying public needs. As of mid-1891, the United States had 987 AC power stations as opposed to 202 DC power stations. Two years later, the world's fair would provide another spectacular demonstration of AC motors.

Both General Electric (a company that had grown out of Edison Electric) and Westinghouse had badly wanted to supply electricity for the fair. The committee in charge of the fair accepted bids to see which company would do the job for the least amount of money.

On May 22, 1892, the committee awarded the contract to Westinghouse. General Electric was determined to rock the boat, however. Edison had already brought lawsuits against Westinghouse and other companies, claiming that they infringed on his patents for the incandescent lightbulb. If Edison won the suits, Westinghouse would be forced to stop making lightbulbs—and thus couldn't supply lighting for the fair.

LIGHTBULB WARS

Westinghouse knew there was a good chance that Edison's claims would hold up in court, so he set his staff to work developing a lightbulb that would not infringe on Edison's patents. A patent Westinghouse already owned for a two-piece bulb, called a stopper light, became the focus of intense work. In contrast to Edison's one-piece bulb, which had to be thrown away when it burned out, the stopper light could be reused by replacing the filament. And instead of creating a vacuum (a completely empty space) in bulbs as Edison did, Westinghouse had them filled with nitrogen. Once the two-piece bulb was perfected, he set up a glass factory to begin manufacturing them.

Westinghouse was wise to attack the lightbulb problem promptly. On October 4, 1892, less than five months after Westinghouse received the contract to power the fair, a federal court of appeals ruled in favor of Edison. No company but General Electric could manufacture and sell the kind of lightbulb that Thomas Edison had created. In December the U.S. Supreme Court upheld the ruling.

If Westinghouse thought he was safe with his newly modified lightbulbs, he soon discovered he was wrong. Emboldened by their victory, the Edison forces filed another suit, claiming that the stopper lights also violated their company's patents. They hoped to get the Westinghouse lightbulb factory shut down. But in early 1893, a judge ruled that the Westinghouse stopper lamp did not infringe on Edison's patent rights.

Less than four months remained until the world's fair would open. Getting all the equipment in place to light up the fair was a huge challenge. But Westinghouse remained confident. "He believed, apparently, that most engineers did their best work when hardest pressed," recalled electrical engineer Benjamin Lamme, "and no doubt, to an extent, he was right."

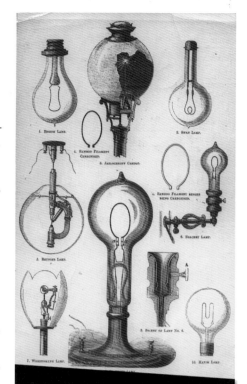

This illustration from the late 1800s shows a variety of early lightbulb designs. Westinghouse and Edison fought a series of patent wars to gain control of the manufacture of lightbulbs. At stake were enormous profits, as well as the glory of lighting the world's fair in Chicago in 1893.

"THE ELECTRICIAN'S IDEAL CITY"

The 1893 World's Fair proved to be the dazzling event that everyone hoped it would be. Twenty-seven million people came to the fair from all over the world. At more than 700 acres (283 hectares), with sixty-five thousand exhibits, the fair was enormous. Few could have experienced all it had to offer. But no one could miss the electrical marvels or brilliant lights. According to the *Review of Reviews*, the fair was "as near being the electrician's ideal city as any spot on the globe."

George Westinghouse, Thomas Edison, and Nikola Tesla joined the throngs strolling through the fair. While Edison enjoyed the attention he received, Westinghouse kept a lower profile. He rarely gave interviews and was not as easy to recognize as his rival.

Of the three, Tesla created the most excitement by giving talks and demonstrations. Formally dressed in white tie and tails, Tesla welcomed visitors to his personal display. Most people might not understand the workings of AC motors and other AC equipment. But that didn't dampen their enthusiasm.

A striking display of copper balls and metal eggs spinning and reversing direction within a rotating magnetic field enchanted spectators. Visitors also marveled at a bright glass

"The World's Fair probably comes as near being the electrician's ideal city as any spot on the globe."

Review of Reviews, 1893

Millions of people from around the world attended the world's fair *(below)* in Chicago in 1893. One of the main attractions was the illumination of the exposition by AC electrical power developed by Tesla and Westinghouse.

tube that spelled out the words "Welcome Electricians" as well as the names of some famous electricians. Tesla, building on the work of German physicist Heinrich Geissler, had made the tubes light up by filling them with neon gas. The gas conducted an electric current between each end of the tube.

Tesla's greatest moment of triumph came when he addressed the International Electric Congress, an important scientific society, which held a meeting at the fair on August 25. Word leaked out that Tesla planned to pass 250,000 volts of electrical current through his body. People swarmed the entrance to the hall, trying to talk their way inside.

The audience clapped wildly when Tesla was introduced as the "Wizard of Physics." The demonstration was everything the lucky audience had hoped for and more. Tesla set spheres twirling and enormous sparks crackling. He made neon lights of all sizes glow brilliantly. And as the grand finale to his electrical circus, he surrounded his body with streamers of electricity. The current only skimmed the surface of his skin, and Tesla was completely unharmed. But the sight was astounding.

In this photograph, Tesla reads calmly as a massive charge of electricity surges around him.

TURNING ON THE FALLS

Back in New York, there was good news from the International Niagara Commission. Right before the fair opened, the commission had decided to go with alternating current at Niagara Falls. Three days before the end of the fair, Westinghouse received the contract to create the power plant.

An enormous task loomed before the Westinghouse engineers. At 1,000 horsepower each, the world's fair generators had been gigantic. But the generators for Niagara Falls had to be five times that large. That meant designing brand-new equipment. As George Westinghouse would later say of the system, "Nearly every device used differs from what has hitherto [up to this time] been our standard practice." It took company engineers more than a year to construct and perfect the first two 5,000-horsepower generators.

General Electric was not totally left out of the Niagara project. With Thomas Edison no longer in control, the company had expanded into alternating current. The International Niagara Commission awarded General Electric contracts to supply transformers and to maintain power lines at the falls. Although this was an important role, it was much smaller than the part Westinghouse would play in harnessing the falls.

A WONDER OF THE CENTURY

Years of hard work paid off on August 26, 1895, when the first Westinghouse dynamo sent alternating current racing from the falls to a nearby industrial plant. One month later, another generator was started. The Niagara Falls power plant was up and running.

Nikola Tesla, whose pioneering work had made it all possible, visited the site on July 19, 1896. He thoroughly enjoyed viewing the machinery and taking a fancy elevator down into the depths of the power station. He could hear the rush of the water and see the turbines turning wildly. Afterward, he spoke to the press, calling the setup "all and more than I anticipated it would be. It is fully all that was promised. It is one of the wonders of the century."

The next big goal was to send the electricity to the city of Buffalo, 26 miles (42 km) away. One second past midnight on November 15, 1896, a

This photograph shows the giant generators used to create electricity at Niagara Falls.

man pulled three switches at the Niagara plant. At the same instant, a man in the powerhouse of the Buffalo Railway Company, the first Buffalo business to receive power, also pulled three switches. The circuit was complete. Power was flowing the almost unheard of distance of 26 miles. The *New York Times* hailed the transmission of electricity to Buffalo as "the first time that such an undertaking on so large a scale has been attempted."

On January 12, 1897, the Cataract Power and Conduit Company held an elaborate dinner in Buffalo to celebrate the event. Hundreds of tiny electric lights sparkled in the lavish dining room on the tenth floor of one of the biggest office buildings in the world. Three hundred guests applauded energetically when the guest of honor, Nikola Tesla, rose to make a toast. They tapped their glasses with their knives and forks and made a terrific din to show their respect and affection. When the roar subsided enough for him to speak, Tesla encouraged the audience to honor the impulse that prompted people to work not just for financial gain "but for the sake of success, for the pleasure there is in achieving it and for the good they might do thereby to their fellow men."

Everyone present must have known that Tesla had unconsciously described himself. His boyhood dream had come true at last. In many ways, its fulfillment marked the end of the War of the Currents. Alternating current had won.

AC AND DC
IN A CHANGING WORLD

Niagara Falls was just the beginning. With alternating current, electricity could be transmitted long distances. With AC motors, electric machines could do work formerly done by muscle power.

By 1900 factories were using more than half of all the electricity generated in the United States. As more and more factories converted to electricity, their output increased dramatically.

Electrification transformed the U.S. home as well. In the early decades of the twentieth century, electricity arrived in more and more towns and cities. Americans not only lit their homes with incandescent lamps, they also purchased electric fans, washing machines, stoves, refrigerators, irons, radios, and a host of other new electric appliances. The new machines changed the way people cleaned, cared for their homes, got their news and entertainment, and spent their free time.

EDISON: TRANSFORMING THE WORLD

After his loss in the War of the Currents, Thomas Edison became somewhat disenchanted with the electric business. "I am going to do something now so different," he told a friend, "and so much bigger than anything I've ever done before that people will forget my name was ever connected with anything electrical."

A General Electric advertisement from 1908 shows a woman turning on a new electric lamp. Soon companies were selling other electric appliances, including fans, stoves, irons, and washing machines.

Despite this statement, Edison remained a staunch supporter of direct current. He spent a great deal of time trying to perfect storage batteries, which generate direct current. He believed reliable storage batteries could be used to power automobiles, but his dream died when automaker Henry Ford

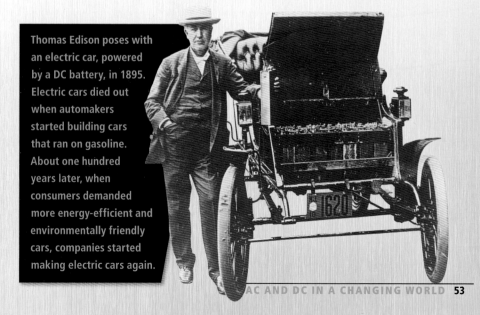

Thomas Edison poses with an electric car, powered by a DC battery, in 1895. Electric cars died out when automakers started building cars that ran on gasoline. About one hundred years later, when consumers demanded more energy-efficient and environmentally friendly cars, companies started making electric cars again.

began producing cars that ran on gasoline instead of electricity.

In other areas, Edison enjoyed phenomenal success. He not only invented the incandescent lightbulb but also the phonograph, the moving picture camera, and many other machines. He also opened the world's first movie studio, delighting the public with his short films. Although he had lost the War of the Currents, Thomas Edison had won his place in history.

Edison never publicly renounced his views on alternating current. But in 1908, he ran into the son of William Stanley, the man who had designed transformers for the first Westinghouse AC system. "Oh, by the way," said Edison, "Tell your father I was wrong." Stanley's son didn't have to ask what Edison meant. The great inventor had just come as close as he ever would to admitting that AC was practical and safe.

At his death in 1931, Edison had received more than one thousand patents. In his honor, President Herbert Hoover asked that all the lights in the nation be turned off at ten at night Pacific time on the day of his funeral. "This demonstration of the dependence of the country upon electrical current for its life and health is in itself a monument to Mr. Edison's genius," said the president.

WESTINGHOUSE: WORKING TO THE END

George Westinghouse, along with Nikola Tesla, won the War of the Currents, but he never became as famous as Thomas Edison. He did, however, win the 1911 Edison Medal, an honor established by colleagues of Thomas Edison to spotlight outstanding breakthroughs in electrical science. The award specifically mentioned Westinghouse's connection to alternating current.

After the War of the Currents, Westinghouse continued to invent, developing a steam engine that would be used in ships across the globe. During his lifetime, Westinghouse amassed the rights to more than fifteen thousand patents and established more than sixty companies. When he died in 1914, sketches of a new invention were found by his body. He was working on an electric wheelchair, to be run by direct current.

TESLA: AHEAD OF HIS TIME

Although he never got rich from the AC motor, Tesla was happy to see his AC system spread across the country. Always brimming with ideas, he continued his experiments with X-rays and with wireless transmission, or radio. He developed a number of devices, including a small boat controlled by radio waves. He predicted that one day automobiles might be directed by remote control. He even designed a death ray, a weapon to send beams of particles through the air with incredible energy. The *New York Times* reported that such a device would be able to destroy ten thousand airplanes from 250 miles (402 km) away. The weapon was never built.

In 1917 Tesla received the Edison Medal. At a banquet held in his honor, Tesla spoke about his childhood and his commitment to his work. "I have managed to maintain an undisturbed peace of mind," he told his listeners,

Nikola Tesla inspects inventions in his laboratory, circa 1910. In addition to working with electricity, Tesla experimented with X-rays, radio, neon lights, and robots.

"to make myself proof against adversity, and to achieve contentment and happiness to a point of extracting some satisfaction even from the darker side of life." He graciously called Thomas Edison "a wonderful man" who managed to get "great results by virtue of his industry and application."

Tesla died on January 7, 1943. Certainly not a household name like Thomas Edison, he was nevertheless honored for his achievements. The *New York Sun* eulogized him as a genius and visionary: "[Tesla] was seeing a glimpse into that confused and mysterious frontier which divides the known and the unknown." The newspaper described Tesla as a man ahead of his time, concluding, "Probably we shall appreciate him better a few million years from now."

For many years after his death, Nikola Tesla was a forgotten figure. Few people knew about his contributions to modern technology. Most people associated electric lighting with Thomas Edison. People hailed Italian Guglielmo Marconi as the inventor of the radio, even though Tesla filed radio patents that predated those of Marconi.

COMEBACKS

In the twenty-first century, Nikola Tesla is making a comeback. He has showed up as the character of an eccentric genius in a 2006 movie called *The Prestige*,

Musician and actor David Bowie played Tesla in the 2006 movie *The Prestige*.

as well as in the video game *Dark Void.* The founders of Tesla Motors, makers of electric cars, named their company in his honor. The Nikola Tesla Inventors Club of Philadelphia includes online members from all over the world. Larry Page, who cofounded the search engine Google, also claims Tesla as an early influence and inspiration.

In the modern world, alternating current continues to travel long distances to provide electricity to homes and businesses. But new uses for electricity have evolved. The electronic age has brought in a host of gadgets that can operate without being plugged into an electric socket, such as cell phones, smartphones, and laptop computers. All these battery-run or cell-fuel-driven devices depend on direct current. Thus DC is making its own comeback. Author and historian Tom McNichol writes that "the Computer Age may well turn out to be DC's revenge." If this is the case, the future will belong to both alternating current and direct current—and probably in ways we cannot yet imagine.

TIMELINE

1877 Thomas Edison begins experiments with incandescent lighting.

1878 Thomas Edison founds the Edison Electric Light Company.

1882 Thomas Edison provides electricity to J. P. Morgan's office from the Pearl Street Station in New York.

1884 Nikola Tesla moves to New York and begins working for Thomas Edison.

1886 The Westinghouse Company debuts its AC lighting system in Great Barrington, Massachusetts. Westinghouse opens its first commercial power plant in Buffalo, New York.

1887 Nikola Tesla opens the Tesla Electric Light Company in New York.

1888 Nikola Tesla gives a lecture on AC power to the American Institute of Electrical Engineers. Tesla moves to Pittsburgh to work for George Westinghouse. Thomas Edison warns that alternating current is dangerous. Electrical engineer Harold Brown performs experiments on dogs to prove that alternating current is dangerous.

1890 William Kemmler is killed in the electric chair, which runs on alternating current. The Niagara Falls Power Company holds a groundbreaking ceremony for a power station at Niagara Falls.

1891 A generator sends 3,000 volts of alternating current up a mountainside to operate mining equipment in Colorado.

1892 The Westinghouse Company wins the contract to supply electricity to the 1893 World's Fair in Chicago. The company perfects its stopper light to provide lighting for the fair.

1893 The lights and machinery at the Columbian Exposition are all powered by AC generators. General Electric, Westinghouse, and Nikola Tesla provide demonstrations of the wonders of electricity at the fair.

1895 The Niagara Falls power plant goes into operation. It sends power from the falls to the city of Buffalo, New York, 26 miles (42 km) away—a record distance. The event marks the unofficial end of the War of the Currents, with AC as the winner.

GLOSSARY

alternating current: electric current that changes direction many times per second as it travels over wire

arc lamp: a lamp that sends a strong electric current leaping between two carbon sticks. The current gives off an intensely bright light.

commutator: a device that converts alternating current into direct current

conductor: a substance that transmits electricity

current: a flow of electricity

direct current: electric current that does not change direction as it travels over wire

dynamo: a machine that converts mechanical energy into electricity; also called a generator

filament: a threadlike wire in a lightbulb that glows as it transmits electric current

generator: a machine that converts mechanical energy into electricity; formerly called a dynamo

incandescence: light and heat produced by the flow of electricity

magnetic field: an area of force produced by an electric current

transformer: a machine that increases or decreases the voltage of alternating current

turbine: a device that is rotated by a moving force, such as water, wind, or steam. A moving turbine can provide power for an electrical generator.

voltage: a force that causes electric current to flow

LERNER

SOURCE

Expand learning beyond the printed book. Download free, complementary educational resources for this book from our website, www.lerneresource.com.

SOURCE NOTES

5 Jane Brox, *Brilliant: The Evolution of Artificial Light* (Boston: Houghton Mifflin Harcourt, 2010), 131.

5 Jill Jonnes, *Empires of Light: Edison, Tesla, and Westinghouse and the Race to Electrify the World* (New York: Random House, 2003), 265.

6 Ibid., 270.

6 Ibid.

10 Ronald W. Clark, *Edison: The Man Who Made the Future* (New York: G. P. Putnam's Sons, 1977), 88.

11 Ibid.

11 Ibid.

12 Jonnes, *Empires of Light*, 71.

13 Tom McNichol, *AC/DC: The Savage Tale of the First Standards War* (San Francisco: Jossey-Bass, 2006), 61.

14–15 Jonnes, *Empires of Light*, 81.

15 Clark, *Edison*, 139.

15 Ibid.

15 Ibid.

15 Jonnes, *Empires of Light*, 85.

17 Nikola Tesla, *My Inventions: The Autobiography of Nikola Tesla* (Miami: BN Publishing, 2007), 53.

19 Ibid., 57.

19 Ibid.

20 Ibid., 67.

21 Ibid., 68.

21 Ibid.

21 Nikola Tesla, "Some Personal Recollections," *Scientific American*, June 5, 1915, http://www.tfcbooks .com/tesla/1915-06-05.htm (February 15, 2010).

22 Brox, *Brilliant*, 125.

22 Ibid.

22 Marc J. Seifer, *Wizard: The Life and Times of Nikola Tesla* (New York: Citadel Press, 1998), 39.

23 Ibid., 41.

28 Jonnes, *Empires of Light*, 134.

29 Richard Moran, *Executioner's Current: Thomas Edison, George Westinghouse, and the Invention of the Electric Chair* (New York: Vintage Books, 2002), 52.

29 Ibid.

29 Ibid., 54.

29 Ibid.

31 Moran, *Executioner's Current*, 57.

31 Jonnes, *Empires of Light*, 137.

33 Moran, *Executioner's Current*, 75.

34 McNichol, *AC/DC*, 84.

34 Ibid., 85.

36 Jonnes, *Empires of Light*, 167.

36 Ibid., 167–168.

36 Jonnes, *Empires of Light*, 168.

37 Ibid.

37 McNichol, *AC/DC*, 91.

38 Moran, *Executioner's Current*, 99.

38 Thomas P. Hughes, "Harold P. Brown and the Executioner's Current: An Incident in the AC-DC Controversy," *Business History Review* 32(2): 148.

39 Jonnes, *Empires of Light*, 177.

39 Hughes, "Harold P. Brown," 158.

40 Jonnes, *Empires of Light*, 195.

40 Ibid., 195–196.

40 Ibid., 197.

41 McNichol, *AC/DC*, 124.

41 James F. Penrose, "Inventing Electrocution." *Invention and Technology*, 1994, http://www .americanheritage.com/articles /magazine/it/1994/4/1994_4_34 _print.shtml (March 1, 2010).

43 Jonnes, *Empires of Light*, 213.

43 Moran, *Executioner's Current*, 105.

45 McNichol, *AC/DC*, 140.

47 Quentin R. Skrabec Jr., *George Westinghouse: Gentle Genius* (New York: Algora Publishing, 2007), 140.

47 Jonnes, *Empires of Light*, 265.

48 Ibid.

49 Seifer, *Wizard*, 121.

50 Jonnes, *Empires of Light*, 306.

50 Ibid., 326.

51 *New York Times*, "Niagara's Power in Buffalo," November 17, 1896.

51 Jonnes, *Empires of Light*, 332.

53 Moran, *Executioner's Current*, 223.

54 McNichol, *AC/DC*, 170.

54 Brox, *Brilliant*, 186.

55–56 Margaret Cheney, *Tesla: Man Out of Time* (New York: Simon & Schuster, 1981), 271.

56 Ibid., 270.

56 Seifer, *Wizard*, 445.

57 McNichol, *AC/DC*, 177.

SELECTED BIBLIOGRAPHY

Brox, Jane. *Brilliant: The Evolution of Artificial Light*. Boston: Houghton Mifflin Harcourt, 2010.

Israel, Paul. *Edison: A Life of Adventure*. New York: John Wiley & Sons, 1998.

Jonnes, Jill. *Empires of Light: Edison, Tesla, Westinghouse, and the Race to Electrify the World*. New York: Random House, 2003.

McNichol, Tom. *AC/DC: The Savage Tale of the First Standards War*. San Francisco: Jossey-Bass, 2006.

Michaels, Daniel. "Long-Dead Inventor Nikola Tesla Is Electrifying Hip Techies." *Wall Street Journal*, January 14, 2010.

Moran, Richard. *Executioner's Current: Thomas Edison, George Westinghouse, and the Invention of the Electric Chair*. New York: Vintage Books, 2002.

Nye, David E. *Electrifying America: Social Meanings of a New Technology, 1880–1940*. Cambridge, MA: MIT Press, 1990.

O'Neill. *Prodigal Genius: The Life of Nikola Tesla*. New York: Ives Washburn, 1944. Reprint, Las Vegas: Brotherhood of Life, 1994.

PBS. "Edison's Miracle of Light." *American Experience*. 1999–2000. http://www.pbs.org/wgbh/amex/edison/filmmore/transcript/index.html (November 17, 2009).

Seifer, Marc J. *Wizard: The Life and Times of Nikola Tesla*. New York: Citadel Press, 1998.

Skrabec, Quentin R., Jr. *George Westinghouse: Gentle Genius*. New York: Algora Publishing, 2007.

Stross, Randall. *The Wizard of Menlo Park: How Thomas Alva Edison Invented the World*. New York: Three Rivers Press, 2007.

Tesla, Nikola. *My Inventions: The Autobiography of Nikola Tesla*. Miami: BN Publishing, 2007.

FURTHER INFORMATION

BOOKS

Aldrich, Lisa J. *Nikola Tesla and the Taming of Electricity.* Greensboro, NC: Morgan Reynolds Publishing, 2005.

Fairley, Peter. *Electricity and Magnetism.* Minneapolis: Twenty-First Century Books, 2007.

Parker, Steve, and Laura Buller. *Electricity.* New York: DC Children, 2005.

Silverstein, Alvin, Virginia Silverstein, and Laura Silverstein Nunn. *Energy.* Minneapolis: Twenty-First Century Books, 2009.

Tagliaferro, Linda. *Thomas Edison: Inventor of the Age of Electricity.* Minneapolis: Twenty-First Century Books, 2003.

Woodside, Martin. *Thomas Edison: The Man Who Lit up the World.* New York: Sterling, 2007.

WEBSITES

Bakken Museum
http://www.thebakken.org
Located in Minneapolis, Minnesota, the Bakken Museum helps visitors explore the history and nature of electricity and magnetism. The museum's website includes information on exhibits, collections, and special programs for kids.

Biography of Thomas Edison
http://www.thomasedison.com/biography.html
This website presents a short biography of inventor Thomas Edison.

Edison's Miracle of Light
http://www.pbs.org/wgbh/amex/edison/index.html
This site is a companion to the PBS television program of the same name. It includes a timeline, an explanation of AC versus DC power, information on Thomas Edison and his work, and links to primary documents and recordings.

George Westinghouse
http://www.westinghousenuclear.com/Our_Company/history/george_westinghouse.shtm
This Web page from the Westinghouse Electric Company offers a biography of company founder George Westinghouse, who was instrumental in the triumph of AC power in the War of the Currents.

Lighting a Revolution
http://americanhistory.si.edu/lighting/19thcentury/invent19.htm
This website, a companion to an exhibit at the Smithsonian American History Museum, discusses various aspects of Thomas Edison's incandescent lamp.

Tesla: Master of Lighting
http://www.pbs.org/tesla/
This companion website to the PBS video of the same name provides extensive information on Nikola Tesla's life and inventions.

Tesla Memorial Society of New York
http://www.teslasociety.com/biography.htm
This website is devoted to the writings, inventions, and life of Nikola Tesla.

INDEX

PHOTO ACKNOWLEDGMENTS

The images in this book are used with the permission of: © Chicago History Museum/Archive Photos/ Getty Images, pp. 4-5; © W. K. L. Dickson/George Eastman House/Archive Photos/Getty Images, p. 7 (left); © Pantheon/SuperStock, p. 7 (right); © Culver Pictures/The Art Archive at Art Resource, NY, pp. 9, 14; U.S. Department of the Interior, National Park Service, Edison National Historic Site, p. 12; © Universal History Archive/Universal Images Group/Getty Images, pp. 13, 41; © William England/London Stereoscopic Company/Hulton Archive/Getty Images, pp. 16-17; © Laura Westlund/Independent Picture Service, pp. 19, 24; AP Photo, p. 21; © Bettmann/CORBIS, pp. 27, 28, 40, 55; © Everett Collection/SuperStock, pp. 34, 45, 49; © Science Source/Photo Researchers, Inc., p. 36; © Mary Evans Picture Library/The Image Works, p. 42; © Hulton Archive/Getty Images, p. 47; © William Henry Jackson/Field Museum Library/Archive Photos/Getty Images, p. 48; Library of Congress, pp. 51 (HABS NY,32-NIAF,3--5), 53 (top, LC-USZ62-16416); © General Photographic Agency/Hulton Archive/Getty Images, p. 53 (bottom); © Touchstone/Warner Bros/The Kobal Collection/Art Resource, NY, p. 56.

Front cover: © Martin Mulder/Dreamstime.com.

Main body text set in Frutiger LT Std 11/15. Typeface provided by Adobe Systems.

ABOUT THE AUTHOR

Stephanie Sammartino McPherson wrote her first children's story in college, and she hasn't stopped writing since. A former teacher and freelance newspaper writer, the award-winning author has written thirty books and numerous magazine stories. She especially enjoys writing about science and the human interest stories behind major discoveries. Her most recent book is *Iceberg Right Ahead: The Tragedy of the Titanic.*